The Edges of Light

Selected Poems: 1983-1990

Essential Poets Series 60

Hélène Dorion

The Edges of Light

Selected Poems: 1983-1990

Translated from the French
by Andrea Moorhead

Guernica
Toronto / New York
1995

Original titles:
Selections from *L'intervalle prolongé, Hors champ, Les retouches de l'intime, Les corridors du temps, Un visage appuyé contre le monde.*

Antonio D'Alfonso, editor.
Guernica Editions Inc.
P.O. Box 117, Station P, Toronto (Ontario), Canada M5S 2S6
340 Nagel Drive, Cheektowaga, N.Y. 14225-4731 USA

Legal Deposit — Second Quarter
National Library of Canada and
Bibliothèque nationale du Québec.

Library of Congress Catalog Card Number: 93-73685

Canadian Cataloguing in Publication Data

Dorion, Hélène, 1958-
The edges of light: selected poems, 1983-1990
(Essential poets; 60)
Translated from the French.
ISBN 0-920717-95-0
I. Moorhead, Andrea, 1947- . II. Title. III. Series.
PS8557.0748E44 1994 C841'.54 C93-090048-0
PQ3919.2.D67E44 1994

Contents

Preface

The stillness of Lac Connelly in the winter, the deep shadows that fall from its great pines, a banding of solitude and contemplation form a poetic voice that draws its sustenance from the antithetical nature of human relationships. Hélène Dorion writes from the pivotal point of each word. Darkness that turns to shadow, emptiness to hollowness, fissure to fault, disappearance to absence. There is no separation or loss in this poetry; all is held at arm's length or close to the heart. What disappears into the exterior world reappears as gesture, voice, a never-abandoned linking of self and love. The words walk a tightrope across an anticipated lack of response, a half frozen gesture that cannot touch even the surface of another's being. The context of the poems is the human voice. The space the reader inhabits is a lover's mind, a lover's doubt, a lover's loneliness and dread of what lies beyond the human.

At the center of the texts is the person loved: never described, never allowed to speak, this eternal body, this love that emerges from the shadows around us, central to the voice of the poems, loved with constance and unswerving fidelity, pledge of the poems' lifeblood, impression of their voice, their image, their pressing against the limits of banality, daily depression, personal despair. The words echo in the reader's head. Despite the highly chiselled use of language, the almost clinically cold choice of words, the adherence to the vocabulary of daily discourse, the poems offer a strangely calming comfort, a soothing hope for those who question and move through the world with sensitivity and a certain tentativeness.

The act of translating these poems was an extended dialogue between poet and translator. Each poem passed through many filters before it was re-iterated, re-formed, and re-lived in English. The poet's insistence that the voice of the poem in English remain as tightly connected to the original intention of the words as possible, and the translator's desire to 'warm up' the text a little, to bend the flow of the words towards a more philosophical interpretation, provided a fruitful dynamic. Between a word's aura in French and its expression in English are many levels of apprehension and interpretation. The translator had to act as the first reader in an aesthetic garden of Eden and then quickly become the gardener.

The moral frankness of Hélène Dorion's work creates an unusual degree of accessibility for the Anglophone reader. The intimacy of the French verb is given a more contemporary tone. Although the language is not scientific, it is clear that the voice of the poem encompasses a post-nuclear world view. The human is seen as part of the atomic whole with no privileges of form or intentionality. The reader moves easily from the starkness and blunt solitude of *Prolonged Interval*, which is poetically the densest section of the book, into the more open rhythms of *Out of Focus*. The language becomes corporeal and the interrogation more personal. The reader acknowledges the presence of the other, this person addressed but absent. The fragmented relationship, which exists in an eternal present, is given form and colour. The open prose texts of *Intimate Alterations* begin to build up emotional and philosophical density and a physical environment in which the poems take place. The interrogation begins to widen. The reader is no longer certain if it is just the lover who is being addressed. Fusion of the poetic voice with the earth, the experience of nullity and non-being accompany the narrative line. The tautness of the poetic voice cedes to the exactitude of the body in Dorion's portrayal of personal death and disappearance in *Time's Corridors*. The voice grows stronger and the psychological risk of annihilation intensifies. The poems move rapidly between everyday concerns and the mute power of the natural world, of the cosmos that impinges on the human, deforming and liberating the spirit. Once situated in this larger framework, the poems move into a celebration of time, love, and memory. The inner calmness seen in fragments in *Prolonged Interval* becomes the dominant motif. We realize in *A Face Pressed Against the World* that the lover's life is an open text, a letter never mailed but constantly refined, altered, abandoned, picked up. The text is an act of faith in the efficacy of the human, a gesture of the finite towards the infinite, a continual movement from hollowness to love, from silence to expression, from awareness to oblivion. Hélène Dorion does not resolve the tension between love and annihilation, anticipation and fulfillment. The reader is left with a luminous contradiction: 'We have nowhere to go and that is our way, the instant of clearness that greets us. And farther off, the night into which it will soon throw itself.'

Andrea Moorhead
Deerfield, Massachusetts
January 19, 1992

PROLONGED INTERVAL

1983

fissure takes the place
of expression

I explore
                this emptiness
sweats

on the waters
this blue of memories

light traces the assault
wind the grasses
cross the inner walls

alone

the ground
                persists

this earth: motionless presence
and I resist
the whiteness

a shadow leans
gullies close up
suddenly
the eye climbs back up from the darkness

you were outlining the day
on your window
the noise disperses the air
outside
abolishes the angle of your cry

and this fire that was opening
naming the straw
in the dampness
multiplying the decors
where you pass
– where you do not enter

your steps retain my face
I brush against your corridors
– incessant

brightness

that your arm scatters
up to this hand

your shadow
– bearable
farther off
your step re-covered
buried

this death
grasping presence
sharpened

quest of darkness
                    in blood's memory

I have wandered

so much lava behind the nape

the earth
          begins again
under the footsteps
the word takes meaning
                    suddenly
brief glimmers
proclaiming its last collision

OUT OF FOCUS

1985

At that time I had only eyes
absent from myself my body
locked from the inside
outside my paths narrowed
until they no longer were
I traced the erratic
movement of flesh
bound to dark as to silence
I walked at the edge of myself
conjugating exile and flight
from what remained
in the muscles
a fragment of a gesture
knowing well the grasp
of a shadow
not belonging to me

all that is my life you know
this cold that intervenes
to endlessly inscribe the end

I will write only this form
of you under my glance
only your body taming
the cadence of waves the expanse of
paths remembering
us what have you forgotten
if not these words
repeated after me
I love you no longer means
anything
the night I spend
looking for you I exhaust myself
and yet knowing well
somewhere how to consent
to oblivion

What we were does not concern
anyone above all not us
this crease
in the middle of the sheets
you know also
how to join black to black
in a way
with open pores have you
experienced the absence
of my body
did you at least approach

Saying this name I will know
the distress that assails me
under the skin didn't you
forget a few fingers since
this spring which you have all
falsified this afternoon
that your hands retain
my body do you remember
my name which fills the space
as if to overturn again
even more in the very depths
of you

I took the longest path
to myself so many detours
useless pursuits
to go farther
in my wandering I sank
knowing nothing about myself
who was the other
and this reality drilled deep
extracting from my body
what remained of life

Of emotion undergone what do I know
if not the incoherence
of this place where I was
whatever you think of it
both confused and lucid
outside appearances hardly ferocious
according to the expression
that you choose then
it was a day what am I saying
entire weeks
biting into
each one's fissures
points of flight and you know
how to flee better than I

There would only be this day
this way of watching
light break on the horizon
sensing this rising
at its very limit

These remnants of a music
as something that will line up
the glances directed
to the shadow then turned into
dazzling perspective
which transforms your paths
this way I mean of articulating
your phrases your skins also
will move the spaces you
will no longer be anything but this gesture
of gliding towards yourself towards
yourself not holding yourself back any longer

INTIMATE ALTERATIONS

1987

In the decor of the room, you resemble a shadow that becomes what it touches. I see your body and the space it displaces. To elude your glance, I would have to slide into this sea the horizon draws. But incessantly I return to your face, your shoulders, your arms.

*

Outside the road is black. I wait for something to appear, for you to come along the berme of this road. It is twenty-two hours and the blackness hasn't diminished at all. I see my face reflected in the window; everything is half empty.

*

What was I trying to tell you in the texture of the writing? And you, what are you looking for in the contrasting image of reality? You will place alongside my body a body other than yours. You will tell me to withdraw, then approach again. I will walk on the paths you put down as a way of filling up the distance between life and myself.

*

Like a bottomless form, I walk without really advancing towards a place that would gather both your face and mine. I speak to you, silencing the distance that holds me. I think about what's beginning again, under other forms.

*

By what path will you rejoin me? What music and what sign from you will reach me who am a mere shadow without contour? I would like to remember you in a decor other than that of silence. One day I will walk all the way to the center of this world and you will have been waiting for me there, immobile and without other desire.

*

The tree, without my body knowing, breathes. I write across its feints, in the middle of a wind that protects us from ourselves. From the tree, I will tell you the life that is sheltered there, this fragile point between force and abandon.

*

The hours pass and slowly scrape your skin. It is you, you tell me, that I need most. Later we will evoke the unshackled movement of the sea, this wave that, in us, beats down irreparably onto the stone and sand. I will know that we are crossing the same mass of dust and that little remains to live on.

*

You amass so many clouds before me, so many limitless nights. Perhaps you will come by a path other than that of desire, by other pores than mine. Then I will stay there turning upon myself, inventing other entries.

*

Certain evenings, as a way of disappearing behind thought, suspending on my voice the fibers of an unwavering, unbending meaning. Certain evenings, all seems clear, reducible to the simplest gesture. Then the touching becomes skillful, almost generous.

*

You will come by this path, you will tell me nothing has existed since that day when your glance embraced my face. There will be no more broken branches, no more dust on the ground, no more shadow where the light lies down low. There will be only this path that rejoins me and pronounces tenderness.

*

The exactitude of the body consists perhaps in coming back from pain, from that first wave that severed reality. The exact gesture is the one that immobility re-covers. My body faces the sun; I coat it with clay and silence.

*

We need this wind, this tree, this earth to be able to say yet another thing about this world. The place I come from doesn't exist; there is only a ground on which to spread out each of our branches gnawed by the wind. I would like to know only one gesture, living.

*

On the doorstep, someone looks at the emptiness. Without anything really stirring, this body advances towards me. There is in this room a love, an illusion of the possible. A voice untiringly pronounces the same words. I hear crash, cut, rustle. I am naked, face down against the hard, cold ground.

*

To quiet the extent of the weakness; that, perhaps, goes without saying. The imprint of light on the grasses, the repeated voice of the break, the odour of a neck, of those pores where a face topples; perhaps that has no importance. Standing behind another body, I see this flaw that desire corrects.

*

In the room the light dims. We descend towards this blackness. Somewhere else voices are paths that become overgrown. The noise is behind us, it does not cover over what you are saying: I love you. Brusquely, that stops the disorder.

*

The room is empty now. You have reopened the angle of disappearances. My glance, my hand, my desire shed you. This emptiness has the durable beauty of silence and I do not know if I can live on reality's substance as much as on its absence, its disappearance.

*

In the narrowest path of the forest, I perceive you, your body leaning against a tree that resembles you. On the ground, there are yellowed leaves, broken branches. I like to believe that one day the wind will have passed by, that oblivion will have been possible.

*

Life stops. I watch the figure that this stopping corrects. It is no longer said that the earth exists under emptiness or that the tongue penetrating the mouth is a breach. You get up and leave the room; I love the silence of disappearance.

*

TIME'S CORRIDORS

1988

Being able to tell me that time passes in life. Being able to understand that without raising your eyes towards the blackness of the universe, there where everything seems so fine.

*

You are no longer entirely there
you disappear
slowly in me
time no longer means life

*

My death will be like
all others
that upset and leave indifferent
because too far at times

*

You watch the love that yields
under the weight of faces
you gather what remains
at the end of desire

*

Silence is so final
when it comes from you
I set down a few phrases
but it is already so dark
in us

*

There will remain of life only this pain
that stabs the body.

*

I do not forget
that you had torn from me the emotion
of loving you I do not forget
these words — I will come
perhaps perhaps not

*

A house burns and we watch it consume what was still habitable. So many houses burn each day in me, and you know nothing about that.

Time passes and have I only begun to live?

*

In you for months
I breathed without believing
that this would end one day
my breath taken away
from you I came out
without believing it would last

*

I am looking for what, from the world, soaks into me who scatter the curves of absence.

*

Do I have only one desire perhaps
to live the entire universe
through you don't I have only one story
walking from disaster to beginning

*

The earth turns and life
does it know
who remains there
in the empty room

*

Your footsteps hesitant
towards me your gestures
without anything being said
you keep me at a distance
from us you express the gap
and push me yet a little
farther from you

*

I do not want to see the night again
that shuts down the day
in you I do not want to live
absence

*

The encounter knows nothing of yesterday nor of tomorrow. Without listening, you poured time between us.

*

The bird lands on the highest branch. That happens. But one cannot give the footsteps dotting the path the form of the bird perched on the highest branch. That cannot happen.

*

The body in the light of the glance, the instant without fright, the impulse the hand deciphers; these figures of life astonish you.

*

With what body will my shadow mingle
now that yours has disappeared
without deceiving the emptiness

*

The sun sinks behind the earth and I have not yet begun to live.

*

If you were able to feel
this heat that stifles me
suddenly the odour
of you coming back
at the end of the line your voice
and mine disguising this burning
immense as the memory
I have of you

*

Have I ever gone there where abandon was possible, there where my soul could risk losing itself?

*

You will no longer see this emptiness
except in yourself
when time will have killed
this bit of reality
to which you cling

*

In the morning, I would like to be able to seize
the cup of coffee on the table, and not tremble
to know that another day will live without you.

*

I watch you
and try to throw
overboard the images
of this love we didn't know
how to handle because in you
so many boats
refuse shipwreck

*

Outside the wind contradicts your absence. It pushes the body ahead of itself, loads it down with shivers, with desires.

*

Four walls some chairs
a few tables a big bed
you displace and replace
day after day the visible
but decors do not always
resemble life

*

The tree creaks under the force of the wind. I walk towards this tree that has something to say about the human.

*

I am looking at death closely: a cobblestone, a motionless insect, a few desires on a shore. And you who are not there.

*

I am searching for the gesture that will be a path.

*

The thought of the other remains foreign to me. I look at it and love it, always foreign.

*

Who are you? Who am I when the earth turns in me and the wind takes apart my body?

*

I like the wind to tear me from the shore and its skin to quiver in me.

*

When you call me back
next to you
the world has no sequel but love

*

Ruin? A world at the limit of the world, a wall that no longer terrifies. Perhaps also this woman whom the story does not betray, this woman I am, held back by the wind.

*

The night I become
the airplane crushed
in the veins of time

*

The question without terror does not matter.

*

The landscape that has been shaken is the one that renews us. I love the wave that breathes to the sand the force of abandonment and exhausts itself alone.

*

Does one know dust, foam, seaweed and rock? I am waiting for what will lead me all the way to my night.

*

Perhaps am I only a tremor of the earth, trying to disappear. Perhaps am I only that: a tremor of being in the middle of an eclipse.

*

One marvels at so many lives
to seize hold of things
towards what furrow am I thrown
in what black room
filled with fissures

*

I look at the immediate horizon
that surveys the flesh
cuts scattered in me
like reasons for having passed
buried into a story
of love and disappearance

*

A particle from somewhere else and some other time; a provisional desire of the universe; a possible path of time. Perhaps I am only that.

A FACE PRESSED AGAINST THE WORLD

1990

LETTER

Light snow, slow. It is not unusual that the day leaves me like this, withdrawn from the world's pulse, alone enough never to cease being alone. A clearness persists in the depths of the night. Stones, water, sky; a light has descended, doomed to darkness, to silence.

On the table, letters. Fragile traces that settle on my life, passage above absence.

Light snow, as if the dust of the world were coming back over us. So few things often remain: features on a face, prints held by fingertips, pieces heaped up by time, frail fragments scattered here and there, as if the light sign were not yet the sign, a few flakes not yet snow.

Buzzing, droning, day that groans within the day. Far from what is continually withdrawing, I listen to the beginnings that a second crosses. From all angles at once, life is there – irreparable movement of light and shade, right and wrong side of the same season, the same word. Life is there, occasionally breaking on itself. In the middle of our shared banality, I write you, I love you.

Light and slow snow of a night that came to stretch out between the world and me. It is always the same child who returns through us, always the same desire that murmurs – my love, and allows itself to be approached by disaster.

Seen from the window, the untouched edge of the day. Time passes. Like a wound, certain hours come and go, leave me with a look, a solitude that throws me apart from things, from the reality raised by a few words. A flaw stands out across your letters, among these shreds of infinity that our hands, our voices, have reassembled.

Once again the night in the middle of slow hours. In such moments I would love to be able to join you, to feel with you the weight finally supported of the emptiness on our soul, to remain peaceably attentive to the silence thus shed, to seize gently the unseizable.

On the table, your letters and mine, the features of a loss never reabsorbed. Lacking inside or outside, they preserve me from that uninhabitable place, emptiness without a body given over to it.

Our voice continually escapes us, and with it, what one is and does. Among the interminable passages that writing follows, will I find your presence?

Most often, we walk without understanding this movement, without hearing its step, but knowing that we must go beyond an emptiness in us, and that only then our walk begins. In these moments, I think of the desert, of you.

> Suddenly the beating of a bird's heart; that alone breaks the air. Behind me, steps I know I made but which the ground did not retain. I wanted to learn thirst. Sand is this infinity that passes through us slowly ever since a beginning that we cannot name. Stripped of itself, the world restores its whiteness which, alone now, upholds the memory I am remaking. Detached, I am still trying to see if there is someone.

My flesh melted in the desert.

No other event in the night than these slow hours when one strains to hear the least signs of life and when one stops in the face of a few words of love and of despair gathered deep down inside the days; no other event than a silence leaning against desire, and this mad urge to march again, to write letters which do not bring you back.

I am now even closer to hollowness, there, where what one is floats above oneself, fleeing, kept at a distance by some loss or other or in some far corner of the world. In this limitless space, one no longer pretends to be anything more than thousands of particles amassed along time, nor to say anything more than what soon slips our mind.

My flesh melted in the desert, you say.

Light snow in the slow night. In it reappear my weaknesses, secretly sharpened by the cold to which I am held.

Savage and gentle, the darkness that descends in us erodes our certainties. Just that, the non-existence of what links. We do not know what to make of the expanse that inhabits us, if not clothe it with a few words or awkwardly follow the gaps of light which precede us. And sometimes, hold a face against ours.

Your face outlives each sentence set down before you. I imagine you holding one of them as if your soul were able to be consoled by it. I listen to your heart beating across life's minutiae, things as simple as rain on the shutters, an hour or two spent in a cafe, city streets, a poem.

Letters cross no distance; they mix with other passersby in the world's station, there where nothing exists beyond our solitude. There is perhaps nothing or no one, but I persist in combing the darkness and the echo, in relearning everything from a single word that came like an atom of presence on the cold earth. I persist in remaining there where a moment bruises the skin. There is perhaps nothing or no one, and yet your face remains at the end of all the others.

Still the dawn before me, still these letters from you like a corridor where, without appearing, nevertheless you reappear. Your body is a memory of what I am. We have walked up to the room within a room. Like an echo of the air, of a rain shower, of a few stars, we were those uninterrupted passages of life.

From very far off, I lean over these letters from you which nights and days, fissures and relief, desires and losses brush lightly over and over again. Then only, I write you again.

WHAT SOMETIMES REMAINS

Living is a missing face. One must worry about the least body, look for the closest object as if it were a way out, know how to name the hour of a day and the wound that goes through us.

It happens that I close my eyes on life, tired of being short of what greets and lights up. Sometimes I walk alongside a shadow; I no longer know being close.

A glance that skims and moves away, a word balanced in oblivion; also a few damaged objects, a deserted room, the horizon without echo. And always the turmoil in front of what can swallow us, adding what we are to the weight of emptiness.

There are days when one enters as if into an empty room. The hours flow onto the body. Slowly things rid themselves of desires that encumber them.

When these days come back towards us, we then try to throw ourselves somewhere else, into a fragment of memory, a continuous phrase, the cadence of a music. But most often, everything still goes away.

This evening I will not know how to speak to you, write you, make you see what remains when nothing does.

I open a window to the wind. Like the earth, I am handed over to the currents.

The earth, remember: this frail body that bared us, this immense hill offered to the light. Remember the rumbling, what shakes suddenly as if the strongest life was crossed by the most vulnerable; remember a bird's flight upheld by the wind and the grace necessary to touch the ground.

The new air at the end of a day, a corridor enlarged by our steps, the horizon's renewal. Just this resonance of things, this indefatigable presence in us.

What is lacking is perhaps never more than a glance, a bridge that goes from desire to desire and watches tirelessly over the abyss. I am going to love you, place in you my face. These words come among those of an evening vowed to gentleness, to that which asks us to breathe lightly upon the world.

One must no longer walk except within oneself, across those grey cavities, those shadows that in an instant, a single instant, we added to the stone. The window's edge must be an image that retains emotion and carries us back to a beginning.

Something of life has never come; knowledge of the flaw that does not repair.

So that the effacing stops, I turn towards your love. Among these nights that the day no longer precedes, I think of you, of this grey cavity you slipped into me. It is not disappearance that is astonishing, but this way of no longer waiting for it, then even so, one still waits, because always disappearance, loss, its excessiveness — always.

A silence forms and breaks up. We must watch over this movement. Everything stirs, expels and recalls the obscurity.

Who can say what wounds and saddens? A rhythm, a relief, an unexpected upheaval. One no longer knows; one is alone, and yet one can still bend over the shadow, sense a beginning, bury our face in our hands.

A day at fingertips. Always each event, each muscle that moves, each fragment of time accompany us. That alone: a waiting room, metro tunnels, a telephone booth, a beginning of a phrase, the noise of wind or a plane, a familiar room. All our desires, our hopes and disasters are attached to them. We are these daily notations that history forgets, these details balanced from the outside to the inside, these banal encounters that tie us down.

Our body presses against a perishable eternity contained in the instant that is coming. Rustling of the world among the rustlings of the world, I have no other breath but that emanating from a particle.

Trembling with the smallest thing. What haunts and upsets is most often found among common and derisory events: a clumsy word, a missed rendez-vous, a letter never received — something broken, lost, failed. Repetition reaches us like thousands of shocks that make the heart beat.

Thus these words that lie about on the table for months and patiently question me: *Where are you coming from? Who are you? Where are you going?* Thus these sentences delivered haphazardly: *What are you doing? What are you saying?* One of these moments occasionally sinks in us and with it one then continues to walk, to write, to reach out an arm to open the door to one's home.

It's Sunday. Coffee, newspaper, theater; one by one, the hours pass, then the weeks, the years. Living, one finds oneself again without life; the world always has this taste of fright. One watches over the sleep of the other, of this other life muffled but not giving up, still grating, tirelessly lurking nearby — as in this instant of a Sunday standing against the silence where I am going among the anonymous footsteps, perceiving suddenly the solitude riveted to glances, everywhere this same echo of fragility, these pieces of death which, for a trifle, cling to us.

Hail that pierces the day. Perhaps it is enough to let oneself be shattered by a noise of water, of cold, of earth; to feel among our disorders the few seconds that cling to us and overturn the horizon.

I watch these bodies burdened with immensity, too vast for our memories, for our gestures that fright clasps. A limitless space trembles in us, cramped by what fears being born but does not stop boring into the skin.

Someone is no longer separating the edges of the world. Someone is speaking of a wound at the bottom of things and of the clarity hidden in a bedroom, station halls, a date, a smile.

We could live very well
without anything but these daily tokens of
affection:
a postcard in the box, the noise of a wave
the blue on the plain, the words of a poem.
The universe reduced to a few attachments
to the ordinary course
of its own death.

*

We could very well be nothing more than an adventure of atoms
and derisory questions.

One day someone will ask me what I have left
I will have never loved anyone but you.

From a few heartbeats
a light will have re-emerged
crossed by contradictions
I will slip in there slowly.

I will have loved only you, only this promise
held at last by an echo.

On the paths we will not have taken
the seasons will have been reversed.
Nothing will have disappeared, will be missing
neither the forest, nor the stones, nor the void
of hours spent without you.

I STILL DO NOT KNOW

If the wind holds back within itself
    the sensation of the body;
if one dies never being one with the visible;
if there is someone at the edge of fragile days
that traces some limit to chaos, to the
    wearing away of the world
to the darkness that outlives us;

I still do not know

traveling in the strangeness
of a landscape, a street, a continent
or in that of a face outlined by love
and its disappearance.

I still do not know

what this turmoil is
that begins with words
among the most common I write
for you as a road
where one would walk far in front of us.

I still do not know

where I am
with the minutes that topple over in me
nor where you are
with these often banal events
that make history
and do not make it.

I still do not know passing
through a shadow, as one comes
into a hotel room, a lobby;
these miniscule bonds of silence
buried in us.

I still do not know losing myself
in what is coming
and will not come back;
going among these nameless days, these hours
when one finds nothing
to put down of ourselves
but whose mark our hands keep
like unnecessary rips.

I still do not know giving
or receiving this beauty
that reappears in us, for an instant
an eternity that one knows perishable.

Without saying it, without ever writing it
this need of you
of hours that repair the flaw
and when one knows what it is to love
to be loved, to cross our unanswerable
    questions
these moments where nothing shies away
from what we are
and where one is one with the beauty
that borders emotion
and each time plays out its possibilities
through us;

I still do not know

to whom I speak, nor what escapes
from my soul and goes breathing in yours.

If life is not
that towards which we cannot return;
if there is some consolation
for the sadness that comes back
like an alert, the visible mark
of what slowly unravels
in each one of us, the world looks for its beauty
and if it should avoid pain
I still do not know.

Why this shadow, this silence
poured out into our hands
these unseizable absences;
at the bottom of the air, a bird unfolds its wings
and if it should avoid pain
I still do not know.

Will we have time to go far off
to go through crossroads, seas, clouds
to inhabit this world that goes among our steps
from one secret infinity to another, will we
    be able to listen
to the movement of bodies across the sand;
will we have time
to tell ourselves everything and stop being
    frightened
by our tenderness, our common falls;

will we be able to write everything
about the passing of the wind on our faces
these murmurings of the universe,
    these gleams of immensity;
will we have time to find
a square meter of earth and live there
what escapes us;

I still do not know.

LETTER, END

Light snow, slow. Life wrests me gently away from what I am, becomes inhabitable for me, because inhabited. My thoughts find you again. Perhaps you are already somewhere else, in some other desire, some other letter which, secretly, was waiting for you. Night yields to the day and I no longer fear losing myself in these reversals, uniting myself with each one of the particles that a second emits.

I have written you, one last time. I spoke of a wound in us and deep down inside things; of its banality, of the impossibility of closing our eyes, of not seeing in these few words – love, fissure, distress – our shared and intimate humanity.

Snow light and slow. Something keeps us in the distance as in an unalterable, sovereign desolation.

Someone comes and goes, leaves us with these walls still standing, these paths split apart, these bodies filled with unused cells, with crevices where our hopes disappear. Someone comes, abandons us. Only life lasts, in collusion with the day and night; only this bit of landscape remains to which we are tied down as to a voice which makes the heart beat.

We will perhaps never know the inner secret of a second that wounds or heals another second; perhaps we will never know how to love with these hands of fragile emotions which raise us up and swallow us; perhaps we will live forever with unfinished, lost, unreadable letters.

Beginning of night. Some words remain that no sentence knew how to hold. It remains, this silence.

I walk in the streets. Who knows if all the love letters begun, read, torn up, written somewhere in this instant are not the fragments of a single soul? Beginning of night – I am loving you. It remains, this face given to each thing.

Light snow in the slow night. Each letter eases your absence, but it is so little to contain what still summons you, this desire without origin or end.

The mountains, the lake, clouds; all is silent before me, everything overwhelms me and goes, indifferent, beyond my joys and most derisory torments.

Nowhere to go: the only path we know. Well before writing you this letter, I carried with me its disaster and its greatness, the possibility of calling love what goes as far as the eye can see and disappears behind the horizon.

We are walking towards fugitive truths, never searching except to find again a promised soul, to save a little of this world that goes away each time with a face. We have nowhere to go and that is our way, the instant of clearness that greets us.

And farther off, the night into which it will soon throw itself.

Postface

Fixing the Fractions

Born in Quebec in 1958, Hélène Dorion's first collection of poetry appeared at Éditions du Noroît in 1983 and has been followed by several others, the last three in France and Belgium. Le Dé Bleu also published in France a selection from three previous Canadian collections (*La vie, ses fragiles passages*), sign of her growing reputation in Europe. In France she is responsible for the 'Quebec-France' series published by Éditions Brandes and also one of the editors of the Belgian magazine *Regart*. In 1991, she became literary director of Le Noroît.

All Dorion's books have been carefully planned so as to make an artistic whole. There is, indeed, a unity about all of her work to date which is manifested in two characteristics particularly. One, as readers must have observed, is that it is composed almost entirely in sequences. The other is that much of it is centred on love, principally its difficulties and pain. This is not to say that hers is a biographical or confessional art, however. In her treatment of the subject she makes it the paradigm of the human situation, especially its essential isolation and the rarity of true communication. Because she is less interested in the personal than in the wider dilemma that underlies human experience in general, her preoccupations extend in later work, within this same framework, to an ecological caring for the world and consideration of the creative act.

Upon opening *The Edges of Light*, we encounter her earliest collection, *L'intervalle prolongé* (1983). Here Hélène Dorion already explores the themes her writing will develop, in a way more abstract than in her further collections. In 1985, she published *Hors champ*, in which the poetry is anchored in the body and recording the emotional fluctuations of a relationship. It is an anatomy, the main thrust of its demonstration being that what we call 'love' is not an unchanging state but in fact the eddying of many different, and at times contradictory, feelings. One reason for Dorion's choice of the sequence as a form must be that it allows her to deal with a variety of moods at the same time as maintaining an essential unity of subject.

It is in the nature of language to freeze what is actually a dynamic process, perpetually in movement. To undermine this tendency of language, the process of love is presented as a mosaic of feelings. One might compare this approach with the use of paint in Impressionist and Post-Impressionist art, the flecks of complementary and opposing colours combining at a distance to give a truer visual experience. Close to, the subject appears dispersed, just as in the individual poems or paragraphs of Dorion's sequences. Though often fine in themselves, their true significance is only appreciated when taken as a whole.

The sum of our life, not merely the sequence

of our emotions, is similarly such a process. It is made up of impressions, often too swift to be recorded individually, just as the body, the apparatus that records them, is in a state of constant change. In most cases what we call our life is a fictional narrative, conditioned by language, linking these impressions together. What causes us dissatisfaction is that our life does not seem to accord with the naive simplicities our reading of literature has led us to expect of it. In order to avoid bitterness and disillusion, the fashionable but equally misguided attitude in contemporary literature, Dorion indicates by her approach that we need to look closely and honestly at how we really are. Then, in place of rejection, we may find our way to a new affirmation and tenderness based on, and more in accord with, actuality. The former breakdown of these qualities in our experience of love was not because reality is inimical to them but because we misinterpreted it.

A single theme, that of rupture in relationship, is carried through the three collections published between 1987 and 1990, but in each its treatment is from a different perspective. That of *Les Retouches de l'intime* (1987) approaches the fundamental isolation of the individual in an intriguing way. It is difficult to tell whether the *toi* addressed here is a lover or only the author's reflection in a window. Perhaps this points to the tendency of partners to project their self-image onto each other. To talk to one's lover is therefore a form of self-communing. Hence the feeling of diminishment in such a relationship, regret at a suspected lack of real communication, which follows from the other partner's doing exactly the same.

In this collection also Dorion introduces a crucial image to which she often returns later. It is that of *la faille*, the geological fault: a break in continuity between contiguous areas. In terms of relationship it stands for the illusion of being in contact, and the pain which follows on not taking personal dissimilarity into account. It is a contact of separate individuals who do not therefore function as a unified 'couple' despite their feeling of closeness at times. Only if one allows for the actual conditions can anything meaningful be made of such a relationship.

This uncertainty over who one is dealing with is also brought out by the verse style at times. The poetry is made up of short lines without punctuation. One cannot always be sure which phrase fits with which, so that there is a multiple choice of meanings, all equally valid. The fault's geological discontinuity is equally ambiguous. In it may be found a richness of possibilities, or alternatively incompatibility of relationship; it depends on one's expectations and point of view. Given that the mind is capable of encompassing such antithetical positions as the verse presents, it is a hopeful sign that the former possibility is the most valid. 'Do I contradict myself?' (exclaims Walt Whitman in 'Song of Myself' — 'Very well, I contradict myself. I am wide, I contain multitudes.'

To free oneself from holding views while always remaining conscious of the relativity of any situation, Dorion suggests, is to enter a fullness that transcends the miserable servitude of self-definition through the taking of unchangeable positions. In a relationship one may be alone *with* the other, but this is not the same as isolation. It is necessary, however, to guard against making of this insight another act of self-definition, against turning it into an act of escapism in order to shield oneself from hurt. Freedom from self-preoccupation, in fact, opens one to a greater awareness of suffering in others. It is this sense of identifying with others, of 'containing multitudes', that Dorion is to develop further in her more recent work.

In between comes *Les Corridors du temps* (1988), which treats the theme of rupture from a more personal point of view. The widening of territory, the wider implications of rupture, develop out of the continuation of the overall theme in *Un Visage appuyé contre le monde* (1990). Dorion returns to her earlier ambiguity in this work. Just as it was never made clear in *Les Retouches de l'intime* who was being addressed, so here the background situation could be one of loss or simply a breakdown in communication. But countering this ambiguity, and a sure sign that it is a deliberate strategy, is the increased specificity of language.

Much effort has been put into avoiding abstraction, as is clear from a comparison of an earlier version of the verse sequence '*Je ne sais pas encore*' published in Andrea Moorhead's multilingual magazine *Osiris*. Vague phrases such as '*l'inachèvement de la vie*' or '*l'oubli répété de la vie*' have been cut out. Elsewhere the language is made more concrete. '*La marque visible*' replaces '*un signe visible*'; instead of the silence '*versé dans nos corps*', we now find it 'poured into our hands'. A more subtle revision occurs in a passage where Dorion speaks of a tree '*brûlé par une pluie, ébranlé par une secousse*'. The final text changes the initial reference to erosion, a natural disaster parallel to that of the earthquake in the second half of the line. On the other hand, the suggestion remains that this erosion may still be the result of ecological crime (others of which are mentioned later in the poem). The eroding rain might be the consequence of global warming, or else of mountain deforestation.

The ecological preoccupation in this section of the poem is evidence of the subtle way in which Dorion highlights the interconnectedness of all our behaviour. If we are truly concerned with overcoming isolation and entering into communion with others, then the caring attitude ought not to be focussed selfishly on a single object. It was this self-interest which caused the breakdown of the relationship in the first place. The fault in the earth which swallows all of our self-interested endeavours is of our own making. It can only be bridged by a wider, more holistic approach.

On a human level we might begin with recognition of our basic kinship. It is from the realization of the fragility of our lives, at the mercy of barely understood natural forces, that mutual need arises. In isolation we are without significance and only find it in a balance of giving and understanding. From an existence of unreflecting habit which reduces life to the unmeaning level of the briefest